JASON AND THE GOLDEN FLEECE

JASON AND THE

OXFORD ENGLISH PICTURE READERS
COLOUR EDITION

GOLDEN FLEECE

Retold by RONALD D.K. STORER
Illustrated by DON POTTINGER

KUALA LUMPUR
OXFORD UNIVERSITY PRESS
SINGAPORE JAKARTA HONG KONG

Oxford University Press

OXFORD LONDON GLASGOW NEW YORK
TORONTO MELBOURNE WELLINGTON CAPE TOWN
IBADAN NAIROBI DAR ES SALAAM LUSAKA ADDIS ABABA
KUALA LUMPUR SINGAPORE JAKARTA HONG KONG TOKYO
DELHI BOMBAY CALCUTTA MADRAS KARACHI

© *Oxford University Press 1963*
First colour edition 1971
Second impression in Malaysia 1977

ISBN 0 19 580080 X

Printed in Malaysia by Mun Sun Press, Shah Alam
Published by Oxford University Press, 3, Jalan 13/3,
Petaling Jaya, Selangor, Malaysia

Contents

Chapter 1

JASON AND THE CENTAUR

This is King Aeson. He was King of Iolcus in Greece a long time ago.

He had a baby son called Jason. When he was small, Jason slept in his cradle in the palace.

King Aeson looked at his son and said. 'One day Jason will be King of Iolcus. He will be good, and strong, and brave.'

King Aeson had a brother called Pelias.
Pelias was jealous of Aeson and wanted to
be King himself.

So one night he crept into the palace with
his soldiers when his brother Aeson was
asleep, and took him prisoner.

'Now I shall be King,' said Pelias, 'and
Aeson will be my prisoner.'

Jason's nurse saw Pelias and his soldiers break into the palace.

'Pelias has taken Aeson prisoner,' she thought, 'and he will take Jason.'

Quickly the nurse took Jason out of his cradle, and ran out of the palace. Nobody saw her go.

She carried Jason through the forests and over the mountains. At last she reached the cave where Chiron lived.

Chiron was a centaur. He was half man and half horse.

Jason lived with the centaur in a cave in the mountains.

When Jason grew up, the centaur showed him how to hunt animals in the forest. Chiron also showed Jason how to use a spear and a shield.

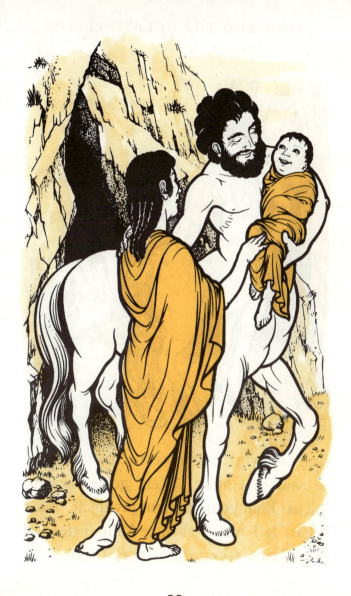

One day, when Jason was twenty years old, he said to Chiron, 'I am going back to Iolcus. I am going to fight my uncle, King Pelias. If I win, I shall be King instead of him.' Jason set out to walk to Iolcus.

Pelias was a bad King, and the people did not like him.

The people of Iolcus said, 'King Pelias will not be King of Iolcus for ever. One day a young man will come to Iolcus. He will be wearing only one sandal, and he will be the real King.'

Chapter 2

THE MAN WITH ONE SANDAL

Jason walked over the mountains and through the forests. He wore a leopard's skin over his shoulders, and he carried a spear in each hand.

Soon Jason reached a river. He saw a
little old woman sitting on the bank.
'Please carry me across,' she said.
So Jason took her on his back, and stepped
into the water.

There was a lot of mud at the bottom of
the river, and one of Jason's sandals stuck
in the mud. When he reached the other
bank he was wearing only one sandal. He
put down the little old woman, and then
set off towards Iolcus.

The next day Jason reached Iolcus, and he walked into the market place. King Pelias was there. He saw Jason and he was afraid, because Jason was wearing only one sandal. Pelias knew that a man wearing only one sandal would be King one day.

'This is King Aeson's son,' he thought.

All the people shouted, 'Jason is the real King.'

A few days later, Jason went to the palace and said to Pelias, 'I am the real King of Iolcus.'

King Pelias was afraid. So he thought of a plan to get rid of Jason.

Pelias said, 'Go across the sea to the land of Colchis. There you will find a strange garden, and in the garden, nailed to a tree, is the Golden Fleece. If you bring the Golden Fleece back to me, you shall be King of Iolcus instead of me.'

Jason was very excited. He wanted to go, but he knew that there would be many dangers. 'Colchis is far away across the sea,' thought Jason, 'and the voyage will be long and difficult.'

King Pelias thought, 'The King of Colchis is a cruel King and he will kill Jason. Jason will never be King of Iolcus.'

Chapter 3

King Pelias said to his men, 'Go to the market place, and tell the people that Jason is going to bring back the Golden Fleece.' Jason and the King's men went to the market place, and blew their trumpets. A crowd of people came into the market place, and Jason spoke to them.

'I am going to Colchis to fetch the Golden Fleece. If I bring it back I shall be your King, but the voyage will be difficult and dangerous. Who will come with me to help me?'

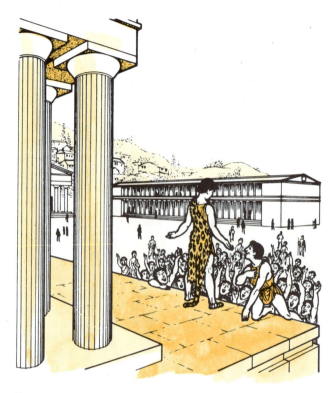

Some of the men in the market place shouted, 'We will come.' Then all the people cheered.

Afterwards, many other brave men from all over Greece came to help Jason.

The men started to build a ship.
The tallest trees in the forests were cut
down, and a sail was made from the
strongest white cloth.
When the ship was finished, it was bigger
than any other ship in Greece. It had many
oars and a big white sail.

Jason and his men called their new ship the 'Argo.'

When they were ready to sail, they all climbed on board the ship. 'It is a fine ship,' they said.

Jason stood up and prayed. Then the men began to row, and the Argo moved out of the harbour.

When the ship was out of the harbour, the men unfurled the sail.

The wind was blowing, and soon the ship was sailing across the sea. The crowd in the harbour waved and cheered as the Argo sailed out of sight.

Chapter 4

THE VOYAGE

The Argo sailed across the sea for many weeks. Then Jason and his men saw land in front of them.

Harpies were flying over the land. The harpies were like enormous birds with women's faces.

The ship sailed into the harbour, and Jason
with some of his men went to see the King.
He was old and blind. He was trying to eat
a meal, but the harpies kept stealing his
food. 'Chase the harpies away,' he said to
Jason's men.

The sons of Boreas were with Jason. They had very big purple wings and they could fly like birds.

They were sorry for the blind, old King because the harpies kept stealing his food. 'We will chase the harpies away,' they said.

The sons of Boreas spread their purple
wings. They flew towards the harpies and
chased them away.
The harpies did not come back again.

The old King was pleased with the sons of Boreas because they had chased the harpies away.

'Listen,' he said, 'and I will tell you how to sail safely between the dangerous rocks near the Black Sea. When a ship sails between the rocks, they crash together and wreck the ship.'

Then the old King told them how to sail safely between the rocks.

'Do as I have told you,' he said, 'and you will be safe.'

The next day the Argo reached the dangerous rocks. Jason and his men looked at the rocks, but they were not afraid. They did as the old King had told them.

Jason took a dove and let it fly between the two rocks. As soon as the dove flew between the rocks they crashed together.

Jason and his men shuddered.

The dove flew safely through, but the rocks caught the tip of its tail and pulled out some feathers.

Slowly the rocks began to move back again.
'Quick!' said Jason. 'Row as fast as you can,
before the rocks are ready to crash together
again.'

The men rowed as fast as they could. The Argo was nearly through, when the terrible rocks crashed together again.

The tip of the stern was smashed to bits, but all the men were safe. They looked back at the dangerous rocks, and they all shuddered. 'The Argo was nearly wrecked,' they said.

The Argo sailed for many weeks, and Jason and his men had many more adventures. At last they reached Colchis, and the Argo sailed into the harbour at night.

Chapter 5

JASON AND THE FIERCE BULLS

Jason went to the King of Colchis and asked for the Golden Fleece.

The King smiled and said, 'I shall give you some tasks to do. When you have done them, you can take the Golden Fleece.'

The King of Colchis was a cruel King, and he wanted to kill Jason and his men.

Jason and his men stayed in Colchis for a few days.

One day Jason met Medea, the King's daughter. She said to Jason, 'My father is a cruel King. He wants to kill you. You will meet many dangers before you reach the Golden Fleece, but I will help you.'

'My father will give you some dangerous tasks,' said Medea. 'He will tell you to fasten his bulls to a plough. These bulls are fierce, and fire comes out of their nostrils.'

Then Medea gave Jason some magic ointment and said, 'If you put on this ointment, fire will not burn you. So the King's bulls cannot harm you.'

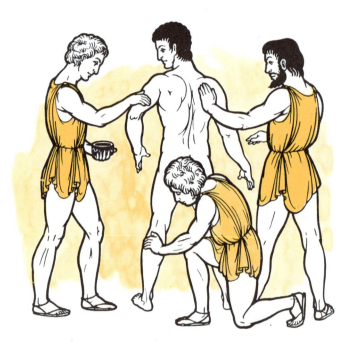

Jason thanked Medea and went back to his men. 'Look!' he said, 'Medea has given me some magic ointment. If I put on this ointment, fire will not burn me. So the King's bulls cannot harm me.'

Jason put on the magic ointment, and then he was ready for the tasks.

The cruel King of Colchis sent for Jason and his men. He showed them a huge field. Then he brought his fierce, white bulls into the field. They were very strong and dangerous. The King could go near them, but if any other man went near the bulls they killed him.

A crowd of people came to watch.

Medea was in the crowd.

The King fastened the bulls to the plough,
and ploughed a furrow across the field.
The furrow was long, and straight, and
deep.

When he had finished, the King unfastened
the bulls from the plough. The bulls ran
across the field.

'Now,' said the King to Jason, 'you must plough another furrow.'

Jason walked towards the bulls. They lifted their heads and bellowed loudly. Fire came out of their nostrils. The grass near the bulls was soon on fire.

The crowd saw Jason walk towards the bulls. They heard the bulls bellowing, and saw fire coming out of their nostrils. They were surprised when they saw Jason go so near to the bulls. The fire did not burn him. The crowd did not know that Jason had put on the magic ointment.

Jason fastened the bulls to the plough. He ploughed a furrow across the field. He made his furrow long, and straight, and deep.

Then he ploughed another furrow, and went on ploughing until the whole field was ploughed.

The King looked at the furrows, and he was surprised. No man had ever ploughed the field with those bulls before. He was very angry.

'Now I will use the dragon's teeth,' thought he, 'and Jason will soon be killed.'

The King's slaves brought the dragon's teeth, and put them on the ground in front of Jason.

The cruel King smiled to himself.

46

Jason picked up the dragon's teeth, and planted them in the furrows. He covered the teeth with soil. Then he stood at the edge of the field and waited.

The crowd looked on, and a strange thing happened.

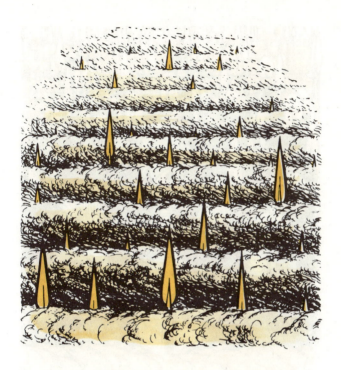

Suddenly the teeth began to grow. First a few spear-heads came up through the ground. Then some more spear-heads came up through the ground. Soon the furrows were full of spear-heads.

The crowd was astonished.

Next a few helmets came up through the
ground. Then some more helmets came up
through the ground. Soon the furrows
were full of helmets.

Jason waited, and more strange things happened.

The dragon's teeth grew into soldiers. Soon the field was full of soldiers. The soldiers were ready to fight.

Jason shuddered, but he was not afraid.

The soldiers saw Jason, and they lifted their spears and shouted.

They were going to attack Jason, but he lifted a huge stone and threw it among them.

Each soldier thought that the other soldiers were attacking him. So they all began to fight each other. They kept on fighting. At last, all the soldiers were killed.

Jason's men cheered. They brought a wreath, and put it on Jason's head like a crown.

The Greeks always put a wreath on a man's head when he did a brave deed.

Chapter 6

JASON TAKES THE GOLDEN FLEECE

Jason again asked the King for the Golden Fleece.

The cruel King smiled and told Jason where to find it. He thought, 'Jason will be killed by the serpent that guards the Fleece. Then I will burn the Argo and kill Jason's men.'

The King did not know that his daughter, Medea, was helping Jason.

Jason set off towards the strange garden where the serpent guarded the Golden Fleece. Medea went with him. She held a magic flower in her hand.

Soon they reached a valley. There were
rocks on each side and a stream flowed
through them.

'The strange garden is at the other end of
this valley,' said Medea.

Jason and Medea walked by the side of the river, until they came to the strange garden at the end of the valley.

There were no flowers in the garden, and no grass grew. Everywhere there were big, black rocks. No leaves grew on the trees. Instead of leaves there were long, sharp thorns, and the branches were twisted into strange and ugly shapes.

At the other end of the garden was the beautiful Golden Fleece. It was nailed to a branch of an old oak tree, and a bright light shone from it.

Jason and Medea went towards the Golden Fleece.

When they were nearer to it, they saw the serpent coiled round the old tree. It looked fierce and ugly.

When the serpent saw Jason and Medea, it lifted its ugly head and hissed loudly. Fire came out of its mouth and nostrils. Medea held out the magic flower and said some magic words. Then the serpent could not harm them.

The serpent moved swiftly towards Jason and Medea. It was just going to attack them, when it smelt the scent of the flower. Instead of attacking them, the serpent lowered its head to the ground. It closed its fierce eyes and went to sleep.

Jason took the beautiful, shining Fleece from the oak tree. Then Medea and he ran swiftly out of the strange garden before the serpent awoke.

He carried the shining Golden Fleece over his shoulder.

Jason ran back to his friends and Medea
went with him.

Jason showed the Fleece to the men.

'We must sail for home,' they said, 'before
the King finds out that you have taken the
Golden Fleece, or he will kill us.'

Chapter 7

THE CHASE

They climbed on board the Argo. They all worked hard, and the ship was soon ready to sail across the sea to Iolcus.

The men began to row, and the ship moved out of the harbour at night.

When it was out of the harbour, the men unfurled the sails. The wind was blowing, and soon the Argo was sailing across the sea.

Before morning, the serpent awoke. It hissed so loudly that all the people in the city awoke.

The King knew that Jason must have taken the Golden Fleece.

Then a servant saw Medea's empty bed,
and he told the King.

'My daughter has gone with Jason,' cried
the King. 'We will go after them.'

The King went down to the harbour with some of his soldiers. They climbed into ships, and rowed as fast as they could out of the harbour.

The King's ships chased the Argo across the sea, but the Argo was faster than the King's ships, and it sailed swiftly out of sight.

The angry King knew that the Golden Fleece was lost for ever.

Chapter 8

THE VOYAGE HOME

The voyage home was long and difficult. Jason and his men knew that there would be many dangers, but they were excited and happy because they had the Golden Fleece.

A strong wind began to blow. The wind blew stronger and stronger, and the Argo was blown into an unknown sea.

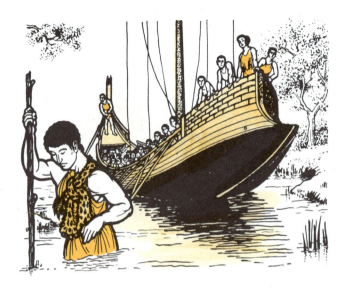

They sailed on and on until they came to a great river. It was long and very wide. The Argo sailed up the long, wide river for many weeks. Then the river became smaller and smaller until it was too shallow for the big ship.

'The river is too shallow for the Argo,' said Jason. 'We must drag the ship overland.'

The ship was very heavy, and the men had to use ropes and rollers to drag it. They made the rollers out of tree trunks, and put them under the ship.

After this they had to carry the Argo over huge mountains. It was a difficult task. The ship was very heavy, and the men were tired.

They carried the ship many miles until they reached another great river.

They sailed down the great river, and came to a land where they saw enormous white bears.

Jason and his men sailed on and on until they came to another sea.

The Argo sailed across the sea again for many months, and one day the men heard a lovely song. On a rock in front of them they saw the sirens. The sirens looked like birds with women's heads and faces. They wanted Jason's men to go ashore and listen to their song.

'Do not listen to their lovely song,' said Medea. 'If you go ashore the sirens will kill you. They kill everybody who goes ashore.'

Then Orpheus, one of Jason's men, began to sing. He sang an even lovelier song, and the men listened to his song instead.

The sirens were angry because the men
listened to Orpheus' lovely song and did
not go ashore.

They flew wildly into the sea, and were
changed into little rocks.

At last the Argo reached Iolcus.
Crowds of people went down to the harbour to meet Jason and his men. Everybody cheered as the ship sailed into the harbour. They cheered again when they saw Jason holding the Golden Fleece.

All this time Jason's father had been in prison. So Jason went at once to the prison and took his father, Aeson away.

Then he went to King Pelias and showed him the Golden Fleece. When the King saw this, he knew that Jason was too strong and clever for him. He was afraid, and he ran away from Iolcus. So Jason became King.

The people liked King Jason because he was very brave and good.